AWESOME OSTRICHES/ AVESTRUCES INCREÍBLES

By Ryan Nagelhout   Traducción al español: Eduardo Alamán

Gareth Stevens
Publishing

Please visit our website, www.garethstevens.com. For a free color catalog of all our high-quality books, call toll free 1-800-542-2595 or fax 1-877-542-2596.

Library of Congress Cataloging-in-Publication Data

Nagelhout, Ryan.
Awesome ostriches = Avestruces increíbles / by Ryan Nagelhout.
   p. cm. — (Great big animals = Superanimales)
Parallel title: Avestruces increíbles
In English and Spanish.
Includes index.
ISBN 978-1-4339-9450-0 (library binding)
1. Ostriches—Juvenile literature. 2. Flightless birds—Juvenile literature. I. Nagelhout, Ryan II. Title. III. Title:
Avestruces increíbles.
QL696.S9 N34 2013
598.524–dc23

First Edition

Published in 2014 by
Gareth Stevens Publishing
111 East 14th Street, Suite 349
New York, NY 10003

Editor: Ryan Nagelhout
Designer: Sarah Liddell

Photo credits: Cover, p. 1 Four Oaks/Shutterstock.com; pp. 5, 9 Sergei25/Shutterstock.com; p. 7 Dhoxax/ Shutterstock.com; p. 11 Elenarts/Shutterstock.com; p. 13 Zagorulko Anton/Shutterstock.com; p. 15 John Camemolia/Shutterstock.com; p. 17 Anup Shah/Taxi/Getty Images; p. 19 nadi555/Shutterstock.com; p. 21 EcoPrint/Shutterstock.com; p. 23 Andreas G. Karelias/Shutterstock.com.

Printed in the United States of America

CPSIA compliance information: Batch #CS13GS: For further information contact Gareth Stevens, New York, New York at 1-800-542-2595.

Contents

Contenido

An ostrich is huge!

¡Los avestruces son enormes!

It is the biggest bird
in the world.

Son las aves más
grandes del mundo.

It grows up to 9 feet tall.

Pueden medir hasta
9 pies de altura.

9

It has a long neck.

Tienen un largo cuello.

It can't fly!
Its wings help it run.

Los avestruces no
pueden volar.
Sus alas los ayudan
a correr.

13

It runs very fast.

Los avestruces son muy rápidos.

It kicks things when
in danger.

Los avestruces patean
cuando están
en peligro.

Each foot has two toes.

Tienen dos dedos en cada pie.

Each foot has two toes.

Tienen dos dedos en cada pie.

19

It lives in a group.
This is called a herd.

Los avestruces viven
en grupos.
Estos grupos
se llaman manadas.

It eats plants and seeds.

Los avestruces comen
plantas y semillas.

Words to Know/
Palabras que debes saber

neck/
(el) cuello

toes/
(los) dedos del pie

wings/
(las) alas

Index / Índice

24